THE ULTIMATE 10

Natural Disasters

TORNADOES

By Anna Prokos

Gareth Stevens
Publishing

Please visit our web site at www.garethstevens.com.
For a free catalog describing Gareth Stevens Publishing's list of high-quality books,
call 1-800-542-2595 (USA) or 1-800-387-3178 (Canada).
Gareth Stevens Publishing's fax: 1-877-542-2596

Library of Congress Cataloging-in-Publication Data
Prokos, Anna.
    Tornadoes / by Anna Prokos.
        p. cm. — (Ultimate 10 : natural disasters)
    Includes bibliographical references and index.
    ISBN-13: 978-0-8368-9153-9 (lib. bdg. : alk. paper)
    ISBN-10: 0-8368-9153-8 (lib. bdg. : alk. paper)
    1. Tornadoes—Juvenile literature. I. Title.
QC955.2.P76   2009
551.55'3—dc22   2008018949

This edition first published in 2009 by
Gareth Stevens Publishing
A Weekly Reader® Company
1 Reader's Digest Rd.
Pleasantville, NY 10570-7000 USA

Copyright © 2009 by Gareth Stevens, Inc.

Senior Managing Editor: Lisa M. Herrington
Senior Editor: Brian Fitzgerald
Creative Director: Lisa Donovan
Senior Designer: Keith Plechaty
Photo Researcher: Charlene Pinckney
Special thanks to Joann Jovinelly

Numbers of deaths and injuries from natural disasters vary from source to source, particularly for disasters that struck long ago. The figures included in this book are based on the best information available from the most reliable sources.

Picture credits:
Key: t = top, c = center, b = bottom, l = left, r = right
Cover, title page: Gene Rhoden/Weatherpix.com; pp. 4–5: Wayne Hanna/AP; p. 7: David L. Nelson/AFP/Getty Images
(both); p. 8: Gary Hincks/Weekly Reader; p. 9: (t) © Rafiqur Rahman/Reuters/Corbis; (b) © Bettmann/Corbis; p. 11:
(t) © Bettmann/Corbis, (b) Courtesy Green County Public Library, Xenia, Ohio; p. 12: University of Chicago/AP; p. 13:
Courtesy Green County Public Library, Xenia, Ohio (both); p. 15: (t) Charlie Riedel/AP, (b) Orlin Wagner/AP; p. 16: (t)
Leigh Haeger/Weekly Reader, (b) Jim Watson/AFP/Getty Images; p. 17: (t) From the Collection of S.D. Flora/NOAA, (b)
Orlin Wagner/AP; p.19: © F. Carter Smith/Corbis (both); p. 20: (t) Eric Nguyen/Corbis, (cl) Dr. Joseph Golden/NOAA,
(cr) Stan Celestian/Glendale Community College; p. 23: (t) OAR/ERL/NSSI, (b) Hector Mata/AFP/Getty Images;
p. 24: (t) Shutterstock, (b) Jim Reed/Getty Images; p. 25: (t) Carsten Peter/Getty Images; (b) Shutterstock; p. 27: (t) ©
Bettmann/Corbis, (b) AP; p. 28: (t) © Bettmann/Corbis, (b) Courtesy Jackson County Historical Society Murphysboro,
Ill.; p. 29: © Bettmann/Corbis; p. 31: (t) © Ken Dewey, Applied Climate Sciences, School of Natural Resources, UNL,
(b) Gene Rhoden/Weatherpix.com; p. 32: (t) © Ken Blackbird/epa/Corbis, (b) © Ken Dewey; p. 33: (t) Shutterstock; (c)
NOAA, p. 35: (t) The Flint Journal, (b) © Bettmann/Corbis; p. 36: (t) The Flint Journal, (b) John G. Zimmerman//Time
Life Pictures/Getty Images; p. 37: © Bettmann/Corbis; p. 39: (t) Mike Zahurak, (b) Joe Traver/Getty Images; p. 40:
(t) Newscom, (b) Adrian Wyld/CP/AP; p. 41: Joe Traver/Getty Images; p. 43: (t) AP, (b) Mark Humphrey/AP; p. 44: (t)
Christopher Berkey/AP, (b) Mark Humphrey/AP; p. 45: (t) Shutterstock, (b) Clay Jackson/The Advocate Messenger/AP;
p. 46: (t) © Bettmann/Corbis, (c) AP, (b) Scott Olson/Getty Images.

All maps by Keith Plechaty

Printed in the United States of America

2 3 4 5 6 7 8 9 10 09

Table of Contents

Words in the glossary appear in **bold** type
the first time they are used in the text.

THE ULTIMATE 10

Natural Disasters

TORNADOES

Welcome to The Ultimate 10! This exciting series explores Earth's most powerful and unforgettable natural disasters.

In this book, you'll get a look at tornadoes. You'll see why they are totally twisted and what damage they cause. You'll also find out how to keep from being swept up in one!

Tornadoes, or twisters, are spinning columns of air. A tornado's funnel stretches from a cloud to the ground. In the funnel of a tornado, air quickly moves upward. The whirling wind spins everything up along with it. The most powerful twisters can produce winds up to 300 miles (483 kilometers) per hour!

Tornadoes are some of the most violent storms on Earth. They can strike at any time, in any place in the world. The United States is hit with more twisters than any other country. About 800 tornadoes strike the United States each year.

Totally Twisted

Here's a look at 10 twisters that have whirled through history.

 Daultipur-Salturia Tornado, 1989

 Super Tornado Outbreak, 1974

 Greensburg Tornado, 2007

 November Tornado Outbreak, 1992

 Great Plains Outbreak, 1999

 Great Tri-State Tornado, 1925

 Hallam Tornado, 2004

 Beecher Tornado, 1953

 U.S.–Canadian Outbreak, 1985

 Super Tuesday Outbreak, 2008

Daultipur-Salturia Tornado
World's Deadliest Tornado

In the United States, tornadoes kill about 80 people each year. But in Bangladesh, one twister can claim more than a thousand lives. That's what happened on April 26, 1989. A fierce twister tore a 10-mile (16-km) path through the center of the country. It destroyed nearly everything in its way. The twister killed 1,300 people. It remains the deadliest tornado in recorded history.

FAST FACTS

Daultipur-Salturia Tornado

Location: Manikganj District, Bangladesh

Date: April 26, 1989

Impact: 1,300 killed, 12,000 injured, 80,000 homeless

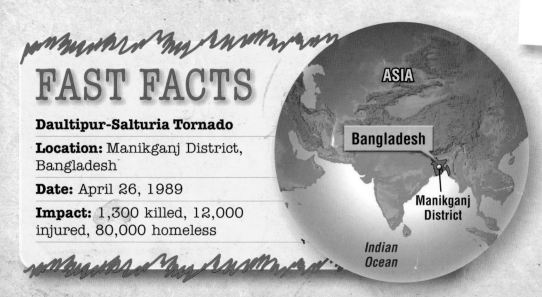

ASIA

Bangladesh

Manikganj District

Indian Ocean

After the tornado, people rebuilt as best they could. A man carried wood and gas containers through his destroyed village.

Twisted Story

Many people in Bangladesh are farmers. Rice is their main crop. In 1989, the country was hit with a **drought**. In late April, the president ordered the nation to pray for rain.

Hours later, people got much more than they asked for. Rain and hail pounded the area as a deadly twister spun through. By the time the tornado lost its speed in Salturia, the entire village had been flattened. About 80,000 people were left homeless.

People were swept away by the fierce winds. Rescuers searched the rubble for survivors. At times, the smell of dead bodies was overpowering.

Eyewitness

" I saw black clouds gathering in the sky. In moments, we found we were flying along with the house. "
—Sayeda Begum, survivor

Vultures fed on bodies of dead animals for days after the tornado.

How a Tornado Forms

To spin into action, a tornado needs moisture; cool, dry air; and **humid**, warm air. Most tornadoes develop from powerful thunderstorms called **supercells**. Here's what happens:

WIND

WARM AIR RISES

1. Supercells form when warm, moist air collides with cool, dry air. The colliding winds form a spinning tube of air.

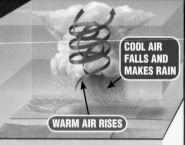

COOL AIR FALLS AND MAKES RAIN

WARM AIR RISES

2. As the warm and cool air collide, they create a rotating column of rising wind. This wind column is called a **mesocyclone**.

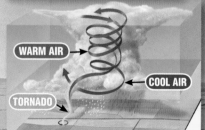

WARM AIR

COOL AIR

TORNADO

3. When the funnel-shaped cloud touches the ground, it becomes a tornado.

WARM, HUMID AIR

COOL, DRY AIR

The base of the funnel appears dark because of dust and other material it picked up from the ground.

STORM PATH

On Location

Bangladesh is in a prime spot for twisters. Cold air from the Himalaya Mountains meets hot, humid air in the area. The clash brings strong thunderstorms. The storms lead to about 60 tornadoes each year. The country's peak tornado months are April and May.

Villagers in Bangladesh stood near a house that was leveled by a twister in April 2004.

Killer Winds

Most people in Bangladesh are poor. Their homes are not built to withstand powerful winds. The country does not have a reliable tornado warning system. The population is always growing, and people live close together. When a twister strikes, it can kill dozens of people instantly.

Deadly Twisters

Here's a look at some of the deadliest twisters in Bangladesh in the last 40 years.

Date	Death Toll
April 14, 1969	923
April 17, 1973	681
April 1, 1977	500
April 26, 1989	1,300
May 13,1996	700

Source: Bangladeshtornadoes.org

Did You Know?

Tornadoes are not the only weather threats in Bangladesh. In 1970, about 500,000 people were killed by the worst **cyclone** ever. A cyclone is the same type of storm that's called a hurricane in North America.

#2

Super Tornado Outbreak
Worst Tornado Outbreak Ever

When more than six tornadoes form in one area during a 48-hour period, it's called a tornado outbreak. Dozens of tornadoes can sweep through several states at a time. Forecasters knew that bad storms were brewing on April 3, 1974. But they had no idea the severe weather would spin 148 twisters in 13 states! After 16 twisted hours, 330 people were dead. More than 5,000 were injured.

FAST FACTS

Super Tornado Outbreak

Location: 13 states in the eastern and midwestern United States

Date: April 3, 1974

Number of twisters: 148

Impact: 330 killed, 5,484 injured

UNITED STATES

Pacific Ocean

Atlantic Ocean

" I started to hear the roar outside. ... The windows to the basement blew in on their hinges. And the backdoor exploded down the stairway. "

—William J. Brock, survivor of the Xenia, Ohio, tornado

During the outbreak, a funnel cloud whirled through Saylor Park, Ohio.

Deadly Damage

At one point during the outbreak, 15 twisters spun on the ground at the same time. The tornadoes spun for a combined 2,598 miles (4,181 km)!

The deadliest twister of the outbreak hit Xenia, Ohio. The powerful tornado killed 33 people when it ripped through the town. It lasted for nine minutes. The strongest tornadoes usually stay on the ground for about four minutes.

The Xenia tornado buried this car under a pile of bricks.

11

The Fujita Scale

The Xenia tornado was an F5, the most powerful type of twister. How was it measured?

In 1971, Dr. T. Theodore Fujita created a scale to measure tornado damage. The Fujita Scale ranged from F0 (light damage) to F5 (incredible damage). The scale was first used to measure every twister in the Super Outbreak of 1974. Six of the twisters were F5s.

Dr. T. Theodore Fujita studied tornadoes made by machines in his lab.

Today, experts use the Enhanced Fujita (EF) Scale. The EF Scale looks at both a tornado's level of damage and its estimated wind speeds.

The Enhanced Fujita Scale

Category	Wind Speed	Type of Damage
EF0	65–85 mph* (105–137 km/hr)	Damage to siding and shingles of buildings
EF1	86–110 mph (138–177 km/hr)	Considerable roof damage; winds can uproot smaller trees and overturn mobile homes
EF2	111–135 mph (179–217 km/hr)	Most mobile homes destroyed; large trees uprooted; permanent homes can shift off foundations
EF3	136–165 mph (219–266 km/hr)	Severe damage to houses and large buildings
EF4	166–200 mph (267–322 km/hr)	Complete destruction of well-built homes and buildings
EF5	Above 200 mph (Above 322 km/hr)	Houses swept off foundations; major damage to mid- and high-rise buildings

*mph = miles per hour; km/h = kilometers per hour

Random Destruction

A tornado's direction and wind speed can change at any time. A twister can whip through an area at random. A tornado may wipe out almost an entire block of homes but leave one house undamaged. The F5 tornado leveled most of the town of Xenia. About 400 newer homes were left standing.

Why do some buildings escape a tornado's fury? A twister can have several strong wind funnels within the main funnel. The funnels can rip houses off their foundations. Buildings that aren't in the path of these winds often go unharmed.

The Xenia tornado totally destroyed McKinley Elementary School.

Did You Know?

After this outbreak, the National Oceanic and Atmospheric Association (NOAA) expanded its Weather Radio across the nation. NOAA Weather Radio doesn't play music. Instead, it issues weather warnings. Today, there are 400 Weather Radio stations on the air. Their warnings help save lives when twisters strike.

#3

Greensburg Tornado
Tearing Through the Great Plains

Beginning on May 4, 2007, a staggering 123 twisters tore through the Great Plains. The outbreak lasted 56 hours. Seven states were hit, and 14 people were killed. Greensburg, Kansas, was hit hardest. An EF5 twister ripped through the quiet town.

FAST FACTS

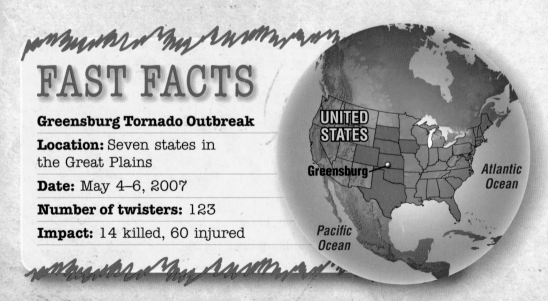

Greensburg Tornado Outbreak

Location: Seven states in the Great Plains

Date: May 4–6, 2007

Number of twisters: 123

Impact: 14 killed, 60 injured

UNITED STATES

Greensburg

Atlantic Ocean

Pacific Ocean

The Greensburg tornado flattened houses and stripped trees.

Twisted Town

The twister that struck Greensburg was huge. Its super-fast winds topped 200 miles (322 km) per hour. A tornado's funnel is usually one to three blocks wide. The funnel of the Greensburg tornado was nearly 2 miles (3.2 km) wide! The deadly twister nearly destroyed the entire town.

Goats sat on the collapsed brick wall of a building in Greensburg.

66 I waited until I heard the roar of the tornado. ... I dropped to the floor and I waited until the storm was over. I was finally able to see that I didn't have any broken bones. **99**
—Emma Faye Hargadine, survivor

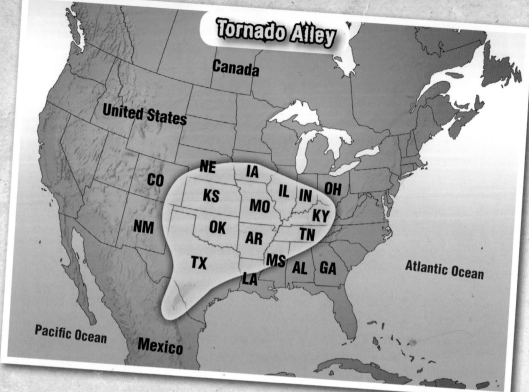

Tornado Alley

Every state has been hit by a tornado. But most twisters strike in **Tornado Alley**. This large belt of land stretches across the middle of the United States.

The weather in the area is ideal for tornadoes. Hot, moist air from the Gulf of Mexico blows into the Great Plains. There, it meets cool, dry air from Canada and the Rocky Mountains. The colliding winds create large thunderstorms. The storms lead to a lot of twisters.

The Greensburg tornado flipped this car. The town is in the heart of Tornado Alley.

Twister Magnet

Greensburg is no stranger to tornadoes. In 1915, a twister demolished a mine in the town. In 1923, people were shaken up by another tornado. According to one eyewitness, three twisters struck Greensburg at the same time in June 1928.

This tornado touched down near Greensburg in the early 1900s.

Greener Greensburg

The 2007 tornado destroyed about 90 percent of Greensburg. Town leaders decided to rebuild it as a "green" city. Rebuilt schools and businesses had to be good for the environment. They use clean energy sources, such as wind and solar power. The government offered money to homeowners if they built green, too.

Did You Know?

Greensburg is home to the Big Well, the world's largest hand-dug well. Its visitor center was blown to bits by the May 2007 tornado. The center housed a 1,000-pound (454-kilogram) **meteorite**. People feared that the rock had been swept up by the twister. However, the meteorite (right) was found covered in rubble in its exact spot.

#4

November Tornado Outbreak
Three Days of Destruction

The November 1992 Tornado Outbreak was a three-day twister-packed event. Ninety-four tornadoes swept through the eastern and midwestern United States. Parts of 13 states were torn apart. The outbreak killed 26 people. Damages topped $300 million.

FAST FACTS

November Tornado Outbreak

Location: 13 states in the eastern and midwestern United States

Date: November 21–23, 1992

Number of twisters: 94

Impact: 26 killed

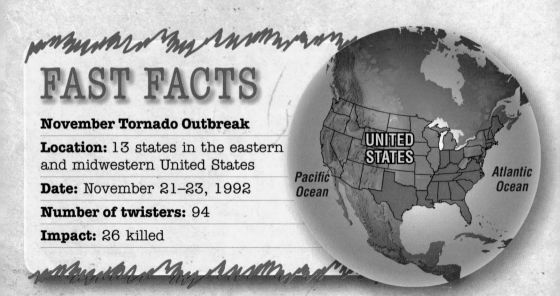

UNITED STATES

Pacific Ocean

Atlantic Ocean

This house near Houston, Texas, was torn to pieces. Houses across the street were undamaged.

Twisters Touch Down

The outbreak began in eastern Texas in the afternoon of November 21. At one point, three tornadoes were on the ground at the same time in the same county. The twisters leveled houses, wiped out trailer parks, and damaged large buildings. In a suburb of Houston, Texas, two blocks of homes were shredded to bits.

By the next morning, the outbreak had spread to Louisiana and Mississippi. More twisters whirled through Alabama, Georgia, and North Carolina. Indiana was hit with 15 tornadoes. At least four of them had winds that reached 200 miles (322 km) per hour.

In a Houston suburb, fallen trees and debris covered yards where homes once stood.

Types of Twisters

Tornadoes come in all shapes and sizes. Here are a few.

Multiple Vortex Tornado

Sometimes, two or more columns of air spin around a common center. These twisters often form in intense tornadoes.

Waterspout

Some twisters form over water. Some waterspouts travel slowly and have weak winds. Others can be fast and fierce.

Dust Devil

A dust devil is a small, swirling column of wind that kicks up dust as it moves. Dust devils usually last less than a minute.

Twister Season

The timing of the 1992 outbreak was unusual. Tornadoes most often hit the southern United States in April and May. Late fall and early winter tornadoes cause extreme destruction. Scientists think that's because cold air moves south and combines with the last of the warm summer air. When the warm air punches through the colder air, a violent storm can occur.

Listening Up!

The 1992 outbreak was huge, yet it killed only 26 people. Thanks to the National Weather Service (NWS), people were warned about the tornadoes.

A tornado watch tells people that weather conditions could produce tornadoes. An average tornado watch lasts about six hours. A tornado warning means a twister has been spotted—either in person or on **radar**.

Tornado Warning

A tornado warning gives several important details:

The area affected by the warning

The location and direction of the storm

Where and when the tornado is expected to hit

Instructions on how to seek safety

TORNADO WARNING
NATIONAL WEATHER SERVICE LOUISVILLE KY
200 PM CDT FRI SEP 20 2002

THE NATIONAL WEATHER SERVICE IN LOUISVILLE HAS ISSUED A

- TORNADO WARNING FOR...OHIO COUNTY IN NORTHWEST KENTUCKY

- UNTIL 230 PM CDT

- AT 154 PM CDT...NATIONAL WEATHER SERVICE RADAR INDICATED A SEVERE THUNDERSTORM CAPABLE OF PRODUCING A TORNADO 12 MILES WEST OF CENTERTOWN...OR ABOUT 52 MILES NORTHWEST OF BOWLING GREEN...MOVING NORTHEAST AT 50 MPH.

- THE TORNADIC STORM IS EXPECTED TO BE NEAR... CENTERTOWN AROUND 205 PM CDT HEFLIN...BEDA... HARTFORD...BEAVER DAM AROUND 210 PM CDT DUNDEE...ROSINE AROUND 220 PM CDT DEANEFIELD... OLATON AROUND 225 PM CDT

THE SAFEST PLACE TO BE DURING A TORNADO IS IN A BASEMENT. GET UNDER A WORKBENCH OR OTHER PIECE OF STURDY FURNITURE. IF NO BASEMENT IS AVAILABLE... SEEK SHELTER ON THE LOWEST FLOOR OF THE BUILDING IN AN INTERIOR HALLWAY...SMALL ROOM OR CLOSET. USE BLANKETS OR PILLOWS TO COVER YOUR BODY AND ALWAYS STAY AWAY FROM WINDOWS.

This tornado warning was issued in Kentucky in 2002.

Did You Know?

When tornado sirens blare, watch out! The alarm signals that a tornado is on its way. Many areas prone to tornadoes have one of these large sirens in a main spot in town.

#5

Great Plains Outbreak
Record Twister Hits Oklahoma

What began as a clear day in Oklahoma changed quickly. By the afternoon on May 3, 1999, severe tornado warnings were sent out. At 7:25 P.M., a record-setting F5 tornado whipped through Oklahoma City. It demolished homes, businesses, and farms. During the outbreak, 65 other twisters moved through Oklahoma, Kansas, and Texas.

FAST FACTS

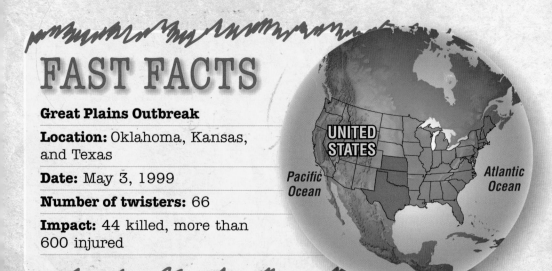

Great Plains Outbreak

Location: Oklahoma, Kansas, and Texas

Date: May 3, 1999

Number of twisters: 66

Impact: 44 killed, more than 600 injured

UNITED STATES

Pacific Ocean

Atlantic Ocean

This outbreak started with eight supercells. Those storms produced 59 tornadoes in central Oklahoma alone!

Record Winds

Wind speeds in the Oklahoma City twister reached 318 miles (512 km) per hour. That was the fastest tornado wind speed ever recorded. People thought the twister should have been an F6. No tornado ever had a rating that high. The twister was the last official F5 tornado before **meteorologists** began using the Enhanced Fujita Scale.

Eyewitness

" The loud roar of the tornado lasted over five minutes, as it slashed through homes, apartments, and businesses. "
—Ellen Cotton, survivor

Tornadoes left parts of Oklahoma looking like junkyards.

Doppler Radar

Meteorologists use **Doppler radar** to track severe storms. Radar stations send out radio waves. A storm reflects the waves back to the station. Computers change the waves into pictures that show the location and strength of the storm.

When meteorologists see trouble brewing, they issue warnings. During this outbreak, the National Weather Service (NWS) issued at least 50 tornado warnings. Their efforts saved many lives.

Doppler radar stations help meteorologists track severe weather.

Doppler on Wheels

Experts can study tornadoes up close with Doppler on Wheels (DOW). Radar units are put on the back of trucks. A DOW team measured the record winds during the Oklahoma twister. They were only a half-mile away from the tornado!

Spotting Storms

Radar scans the sky for extreme weather. But storm spotters check that twisters have touched ground. Spotters report weather conditions to the NWS. These trained volunteers are most important for storms that are far from a radar location. Spotters can watch conditions close to the ground to determine whether a twister will form.

Storm Chasers

Storm chasers do just as their name says: They chase storms! Storm chasers get their biggest thrills from following tornadoes. Some snap awesome photos or create action-packed movies you can see online. For some, storm chasing is a job. For others, it's an extremely dangerous hobby.

Run for cover! Storm chasers often get very close to the action.

Did You Know?

After this outbreak, scientists from NASA, the U.S. space agency, sprang into action. They already knew that lightning strikes often increase before a twister forms. But the lightning can't be seen because it forms inside a cloud. NASA now uses high-tech equipment in space to study in-cloud lightning. NASA hopes its findings will help predict twisters.

#6

Great Tri-State Tornado
Single Deadliest Tornado
in U.S. History

On March 18, 1925, a great twister tore a 219-mile (352-km) path through three states. Most tornadoes stay on the ground for less than five minutes. The Tri-State Tornado that hit Missouri, Illinois, and Indiana lasted for more than three hours! It wiped out whole towns and killed 695 people. This tornado is the deadliest ever to hit the United States.

FAST FACTS

Great Tri-State Tornado

Location: Missouri, Illinois, and Indiana

Date: March 18, 1925

Impact: 695 killed, more than 2,000 injured

UNITED STATES

Pacific Ocean

Atlantic Ocean

Tents

The Tri-State Tornado wiped out most of Griffin, Indiana. Tents gave shelter to the homeless.

Far and Wide

The tornado touched down at about 1 P.M., in Ellington, Missouri. From there, it moved northeast. Most twister funnels are two to three blocks wide. At times, this tornado had a funnel that was about 1 mile (1.6 km) wide! Witnesses described it as "a cloud eating the ground as it went along."

The tornado carried this house more than 50 feet (15 meters).

Eyewitness

" The wind struck the school. The walls seemed to fall in all around us. Then the floor at one end of the building gave way. We all slipped or slid in that direction. If it hadn't been for the seats, it would have been like sliding down a cellar door. "

—schoolgirl in Gorham, Illinois

This school in Murphysboro, Illinois, was reduced to ruins. Sixty students were caught by the tornado.

Speed Limits

A typical tornado moves at 10 to 20 miles (16 to 32 km) per hour. This twister moved at more than three times the average speed—about 62 miles (100 km) per hour. As the twister made its way between Gorham and Murphysboro, Illinois, it clocked in at 73 miles (117 km) per hour. The tornado killed 234 people in Murphysboro alone.

Record Breaker

The Tri-State Tornado holds several U.S. twister records.

Longest continuous track on ground:
219 miles (352 km)

Longest time for a single twister:
3.5 hours

Third-fastest forward speed:
62 miles (100 km) per hour

Greatest death toll in a single city:
234 in Murphysboro, Illinois

Tornadoes can throw objects with great force. This man hung from a piece of wood wedged into a tree.

Back to the Future

Can such a huge twister strike again? Scientists think so. But it would be treated much differently today than it was in 1925. First, the Storm Prediction Center in Norman, Oklahoma, would track weather conditions. Meteorologists would gather information from radar and satellite images. Storm spotters would report tornado conditions on the ground. The first tornado warning would be issued at about 12:45 P.M. That would give people time to head to safety.

Rescuers in Griffin, Indiana, searched for bodies after the tornado. Modern warning systems would save many more lives if the same tornado struck today.

Did You Know?

Meteorologists had an idea that a strong storm was brewing. But they couldn't warn of a "tornado" in their weather forecasts. The NWS wouldn't let forecasters use the word "tornado." They didn't want the public to panic. Instead, the forecast called for "unsettled weather with possible winds."

#7
Hallam Tornado
Widest-Known Tornado Path

On May 22, 2004, a large group of twisters spun through parts of Nebraska and Iowa. One of the 56 twisters was especially dangerous. The F4 twister that tore through Hallam, Nebraska, was 2.5 miles (4 km) wide. It was about 50 times bigger than most tornadoes! The widest-known tornado in history battered the small farming town.

FAST FACTS

Hallam Tornado Outbreak

Location: Nebraska and Iowa

Date: May 22, 2004

Number of twisters: 56

Impact: 14 killed (one in Hallam)

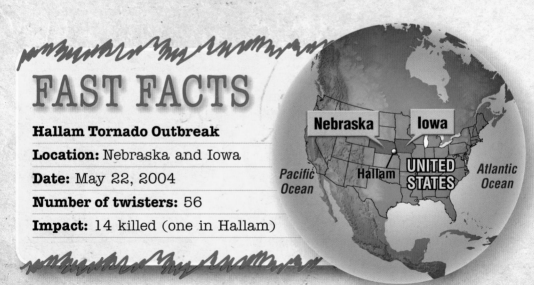

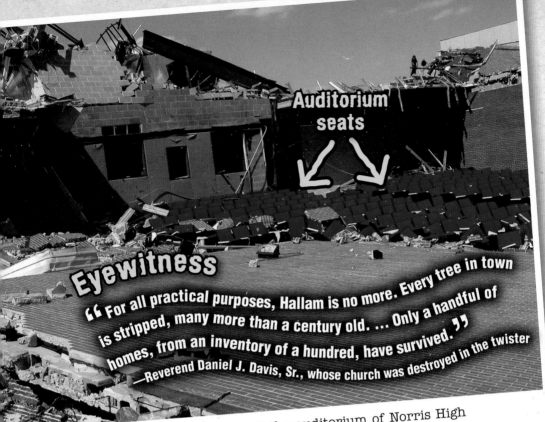

Auditorium seats

Eyewitness

" For all practical purposes, Hallam is no more. Every tree in town is stripped, many more than a century old. ... Only a handful of homes, from an inventory of a hundred, have survived. "
—Reverend Daniel J. Davis, Sr., whose church was destroyed in the twister

The Hallam tornado tore the roof off the auditorium of Norris High School. The walls fell in soon afterward.

Big Twister, Big Damage

The massive twister sped through Hallam shortly after 8:30 P.M. It was on the ground for 100 minutes! The tornado damaged or totally demolished nearly every building in town. The tornado caused $160 million in damages. Only one person died from the twister. That's because people were warned to take cover before the twister struck.

This twister near Beaver City, Nebraska, was part of the outbreak.

Roof
torn off

The Hallam tornado tossed school buses like toy cars.

Heavy Lifting

Twisters are famous for moving huge objects. This one was no exception. One storm spotter claimed to see 25 cows flying through the air! The Hallam tornado also derailed a freight train and tossed it about 20 feet (6 m).

Down Under

Basements are often the safest places during tornadoes. It's best to stay near the center of the basement, not the corners. The Hallam tornado pulled this house from its foundation. A person seeking shelter in a basement corner might have been swept away.

The Sky Is Falling

As the Hallam twister moved forward, **hail** pounded the ground. Large hailstones often fall from the sky before a tornado strikes. A storm's **updraft** pushes moisture high into the sky. There, it freezes. The hailstones fall to the ground before they can melt.

Most hailstones are the size of a pea. These hailstones are as big as a golf ball!

Record Hailstone

In June 2003, the largest-known hailstone fell on Aurora, Nebraska. The giant chunk of ice (left) was more than twice as big as a baseball! Soon after the record hailstone fell, tornadoes pounded the area.

Did You Know?

A record number of tornadoes struck the United States in 2004. In all, 1,819 touched down that year. The Hallam tornado was one of more than 500 that hit in May alone.

#8
Beecher Tornado
Deadliest Tornado in the United States Since 1925

On June 8, 1953, parents in Beecher, Michigan, had just tucked their kids into bed. At 8:30 P.M., the storm's roar disrupted their night. Without warning, a giant tornado ripped apart the town. It wrecked more than 300 houses and killed 116 people. The tornado was the deadliest in the United States since the Tri-State Tornado in 1925.

FAST FACTS

Beecher Tornado

Location: Beecher, Michigan

Date: June 8, 1953

Impact: 116 killed, 844 injured, 340 homes destroyed

UNITED STATES

Michigan

Beecher

Pacific Ocean

Atlantic Ocean

A man stood on the remains of a home in Beecher, Michigan. An open refrigerator lay among the rubble.

Road Rage

The twister moved slowly, plucking homes and buildings from the ground. One survivor woke up about 100 feet (30 m) from his house! The tornado's path of destruction was about as wide as eight football fields. Coldwater Road was hit hardest by the twister. All but three of the 116 deaths occurred along a 4-mile (6.4-km) stretch of the road.

Eyewitness

" We dashed for the basement and just got down when it struck. It just shook the house and sounded like a hundred freight cars going over your head. "
—Nora Cook, survivor

The Beecher tornado was part of an outbreak. A twister in Cleveland, Ohio, flipped this car and destroyed the garage where it was parked.

Stopped clock

The Beecher tornado smashed windows and tossed desks in this classroom. The clock stopped at 8:33, the time the tornado hit.

Helping Survivors

As word of the twister spread, volunteers rushed to help. The National Guard and state troopers searched for victims. The Red Cross handled 12,000 messages from people who were worried about friends and family. The Salvation Army set up medical and supply tents. They also served food to rescue crews and victims. In one day, one group served 112 pounds (51 kg) of hot dogs, 1,800 doughnuts, and 4,000 sandwiches.

Within days, tons of clothing arrived at the area. Many people had been left with just the clothes on their backs. They were relieved to get the aid.

The large group effort to help rebuild Beecher was called Operation Tornado.

Sister Twisters

The day after the Beecher tornado, a twister hit Worcester, Massachusetts. The sister twisters were created by the same storm system. The Worcester tornado was the worst to ever hit New England. It killed 94 people and injured 1,300 more. At the time, it was the costliest tornado in U.S. history.

The Worcester tornado reduced many homes to matchsticks.

Did You Know?

Some members of the U.S. government blamed atomic bomb testing for the Beecher and Worcester tornadoes. Meteorologists proved that only severe weather was to blame.

#9

U.S.-Canadian Outbreak
Most Damaging Outbreak in Two Countries

On May 31, 1985, kids celebrated the end of the school year in many parts of Ohio and Pennsylvania. Their joy soon changed to terror. Shortly after 4 P.M., the National Weather Service (NWS) issued a severe thunderstorm warning. At the same time, huge twisters formed in parts of Canada. Tornadoes soon whirled up Ohio, Pennsylvania, and New York. More than four hours of destruction followed. In the end, 88 people in two countries were killed.

FAST FACTS

U.S.-Canadian Outbreak

Location: Ohio, Pennsylvania, New York, and Ontario, Canada

Date: May 31, 1985

Number of twisters: 41

Impact: 88 killed, 1,047 injured

CANADA

UNITED STATES

Pacific Ocean

Atlantic Ocean

An F5 tornado passed over Niles, Ohio.

On the Move

The first tornado warning went out at 5:13 P.M. from the NWS office in Erie, Pennsylvania. A tornado had been spotted. The people of the nearby town of Albion had less than two minutes to find safety. A twister was rushing head-on into their town. An F4 tornado hit at 5:15 P.M. It destroyed almost everything in its path and killed 12 people.

Eyewitness

" There were the heaviest, thickest, darkest clouds I had ever seen. ... As the clouds moved westward, they were also swirling and rolling. It looked like they were boiling. "
—anonymous survivor

Residents of Albion, Pennsylvania, reviewed the damage in their roofless home.

A tornado destroyed the library in Grand Valley, Ontario, Canada. The front steps were about all that survived.

Across the Border

On average, Canada is hit with 80 tornadoes a year. Few people are killed or injured. The twister that hit Barrie, Ontario, however, was no average storm. It was one of the most powerful twisters ever recorded in Canada.

The Barrie tornado killed eight people, injured 60, and left 800 homeless. Another tornado later in the day killed eight more people and caused major damage in nearby areas.

Deadly tornadoes in Canada are rare. In July 2000, a twister hit a campground in Pine Lakes, Alberta. It killed 12 people and injured 140 others.

Myth Buster

Seventeen tornadoes hit Pennsylvania in just a few hours. Many twisters traveled over hills and through valleys. Before this outbreak, experts didn't think twisters could cross rivers and deep valleys. These tornadoes proved that no terrain could stop a twister's destruction.

Against the Odds

People in Pennsylvania were taken by surprise. They had never experienced a tornado before. The F5 twister that roared through the state was extremely rare. There was only a 1-in-75,000 chance that a storm that huge could ever develop in the area.

People stared in awe at the damage to homes in Albion, Pennsylvania.

Did You Know?

The tornado outbreak wasn't the only extreme weather in the United States in May 1985. That same week, huge snowstorms blew through Colorado. Softball-size hail pelted the Midwest. In Texas, temperatures soared to 100° Fahrenheit (37° Celsius).

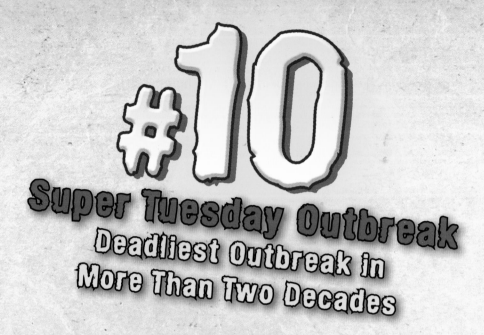

#10

Super Tuesday Outbreak
Deadliest Outbreak in More Than Two Decades

February 5, 2008, was called Super Tuesday. People in 24 states headed to the polls to vote in presidential primary elections. Polls in five states had to close early. Severe thunderstorms were forming. Then, a surprising winter disaster struck. Eighty-two tornadoes whipped through the southern states for 15 hours. The tornado outbreak killed 59 people. Hundreds were injured.

FAST FACTS

Super Tuesday Outbreak

Location: Tennessee, Arkansas, Mississippi, Kentucky, and Alabama

Date: February 5–6, 2008

Number of twisters: 82

Impact: 59 killed

UNITED STATES

Pacific Ocean

Atlantic Ocean

A tornado touched down in Atkins, Arkansas, in the early evening on February 5.

Tornadoes on the Move

The outbreak was the deadliest in the United States in more than 20 years. In Arkansas, the path of a single EF4 twister was 123 miles (198 km). The tornado killed 12 people and destroyed more than 200 homes.

Twisters killed more people in Tennessee than in any other state. One twister tore a 51-mile (82-km) path through the middle of the state. Lightning from the tornado struck a natural gas plant in the town of Hartsville. Huge flames leaped into the air. One eyewitness felt her windows shake. "The city looked like it was on fire," she said.

Worker looking at damage

A worker inspected the damaged Hartsville natural gas plant.

Eyewitness

" People are just in shock. ... They sat down to dinner at 6:00 in the evening with their family and, at 10:00, they didn't have a home anymore. "
—Tennessee Governor Phil Bredesen

Students and parents reviewed the damage at Union University in Jackson, Tennessee.

The Unfriendly Skies

A powerful tornado hit the Memphis, Tennessee, area at about 11:30 P.M. The twister caused damage to the city's airport. The roof of an aircraft hangar was ripped off. Strong winds moved a large plane about 1 foot (30.5 centimeters).

A Helping Hand

A federal disaster was declared for 11 counties in Arkansas and five counties in Tennessee. Those areas received money and aid from the government to help rebuild.

Did You Know?

After the outbreak, rescuers searched a field in a town in Tennessee for signs of life. They saw what they thought was a doll lying facedown in mud. In fact, it was an 11-month-old baby. He had been tossed 100 yards (91.5 m) from where his house once stood. The miracle baby survived the tornado.

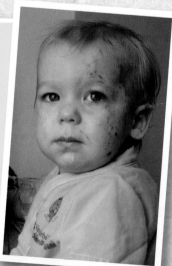

Take Cover

What's the best way to survive a twister? Be prepared!

Before a Tornado

☑ Choose a place in your home or building where people should gather. It can be the center of a basement, the lowest floor, a bathroom, or a center hallway.

☑ Keep a supply kit handy. It should include canned food, a first-aid kit, several gallons of water per person, flashlights, batteries, and a radio.

☑ Create a disaster plan. State where to go for help. Identify someone to check in with if you become separated from your family.

During a Tornado

☑ Stay tuned to TV and radio broadcasts for tornado watches and warnings.

☑ Watch for blowing debris. Listen for howling winds that sound like a speeding train. Head for the nearest safe place in your home. If you're outside, lie flat in a ditch or a low-lying area.

After a Tornado

☑ Watch out for fallen power lines.

☑ Help family members, neighbors, and others in need.

☑ Listen to the radio for warnings and directions.

Students in Kentucky take part in a tornado safety drill.

Honorable Mentions

Waco Tornado

May 11, 1953

An incredible F5 twister ripped through downtown Waco, Texas, on May 11, 1953. The deadliest tornado in Texas history killed 114 people and injured nearly 600. After the twister, experts started the storm spotter program and a national radar network.

Palm Sunday Outbreak

April 11, 1965

Meteorologists were caught off guard when 51 tornadoes struck the Midwest in just 12 hours. More than 250 people died as a result. After the deadly disaster, the National Weather Service (NWS) developed its tornado watch and tornado warning systems.

May 2003 Tornado Outbreak

May 3–11, 2003

In early May 2003, a total of 361 twisters touched down in 26 states. More than 2,300 buildings were destroyed and 11,200 were damaged. Only 41 people were killed during this outbreak. The NWS issued early warnings. Most people had plenty of time to head to safety.

Glossary

cyclone: a powerful, whirling storm that brings strong winds and heavy rains

Doppler radar: a special kind of radar that measures wind direction and speed

drought: a long period of dry weather that causes water shortages and threatens crops

dust devil: a whirling column of wind that forms during warm weather and lasts for a short time

hail: chunks of ice that sometimes fall from the sky before a tornado

humid: describes air that is filled with moisture

mesocyclone: a spinning column of air inside a supercell thunderstorm

meteorite: a chunk of rock and metal that falls to Earth from space

meteorologists: scientists who study and predict weather

multiple vortex tornado: a tornado with two or more columns of air spinning around a common center

radar: a system developed in the 1940s that uses radio waves to detect the location of objects or storms

supercells: the largest and most severe thunderstorms, which often produce tornadoes

Tornado Alley: the central area of the United States where many tornadoes form

updraft: the air that rises into a storm. Tornadoes form within a storm's updraft.

waterspout: a tornado that forms over water

For More Information

Books

Challoner, Jack. *Hurricane and Tornado* (DK Eyewitness Books). New York: Dorling-Kindersley, 2004.

Dreier, David. *Be a Storm Chaser* (Scienceworks!). Pleasantville, N.Y.: Gareth Stevens, 2008.

Faidley, Warren, and Caroline Harris. *Wild Weather* (Kingfisher Voyages). New York: Kingfisher, 2005.

Hollingshead, Mike, and Eric Nguyen. *Adventures in Tornado Alley: The Storm Chasers*. London: Thames & Hudson, 2008.

Web Sites

Hunt for the Super Twister
www.pbs.org/wgbh/nova/tornado/country.html

National Geographic: Eye in the Sky— Tornadoes
www.nationalgeographic.com/eye/tornadoes/tornintro.html

Twisted: A Whirlwind Guide to Tornadoes
www.weeklyreader.com/tornado

Publisher's note to educators and parents: Our editors have carefully reviewed these web sites to ensure that they are suitable for children. Many web sites change frequently, however, and we cannot guarantee that a site's future contents will continue to meet our high standards of quality and educational value. Be advised that children should be closely supervised whenever they access the Internet.

Index

About the Author

Anna Prokos is an esteemed children's author whose first—and only—encounter with a tornado was while watching *The Wizard of Oz*. Although the nasty Wicked Witch spooked her, the thought of a twister ripping through her home scared her even more. Luckily, she and her husband live with their two sons in New Jersey, where twisters are rare.